dedication

For mom, dad and Em

For anyone who has ever needed a friend in the city

Let everything happen to you
Beauty and terror
Just keep going
No feeling is final

— RAINER MARIA RILKE

Any similarity to actual persons, living or dead, is coincidental.

Copyright © 2020 Tracy Huang

All rights reserved. No part of this book may be reproduced or used in any manner without the prior written permission of the copyright owner, except for the use of brief quotations in a book review.

To request permissions, contact the author at tracyhuang25@gmail.com

Paperback: 978-0-578-73955-7
First paperback edition October 2020

Cover art by Dimas Haryo
Layout by Veronica Chin

tracyhuang.online

table of contents

a vision 5
egveni, egvidi, egvici 6
quarantine 7
ferro igni 8
right of way 9
1960 10
my favorite place 11
telephone call from the universe 12
ladies in yellow 13
this means nothing 14
district of ohio 15
girl at the window 16
called 17
chapter two 18
temporary leave of absence 19
studying a new language 20
w.e.h. 21
monologue 22
i, farragut west 23
singsong 24
i want poetry 25
left turn 26
admission 27

phouxir	28
found	29
the cafe	30
satellite	31
home	32
a poem revised	33
order #66	34
understatement	35
revisited	36
conjuring	37
cruising altitude: thirty-four thousand feet	38
unexpectation	39
i could sit on the couch and listen to music all day	40
alignment	41
snapshot	42
in transport	43
ask me for my name (part 2)	44
flight patterns	45
doors opening on the right	46
action item #2	47
birdsong #2	48
the second rain	49
it's all about balance	50
unoccupation	51
can you hear me?	53
blank spaces	54
springtime in the city	55
fo(u)r hours on end	56
one fish, two fish (for alicia)	57
master sun	58
wisdom of the crowd	59
my renaissance	60
not yet/unless	61

a vision

I was told by someone to remember this dream
"When you are awake," she said
And then I was sent away to accomplish my task
Of awakening to the life that I had been bonded to
Yet I could not make sense of this vast expanse
    of space
And the narrowness of the path I had been asked
To walk on, and on, and on, it goes
Where it turns - nobody knows.
And when the full moon emerges to tuck the dusk
    to bed
I search for that woman to appear instead
The vast plain of freedom I cannot bear to endure
And yet no woman appears tonight - no delight -
    I wonder
What's right and what might have happened to her
In the whistling desert of death, next door
Am I dying, or am I simply trying?
My thoughts hang like lonely laundry from the ceiling
In which I count as I lie to and by myself
About my new beginning, which is your middle
Though my ashes have no land on which to settle
I plead again for her to bless me with wisdom,
    courage, or freedom
And to seize me away from this ache - then,
    I hesitate
For I realize that I'm suddenly wide awake

Turning down your own light
Does not help another shine more
Instead it allows the darkness
To crawl in on the floor

The goal that you so desperately want
Needs a faithful guide
And so what better companion
Than a light right at your side?

The path to joy overflows with pain,
So let your own brilliance be our gain.

quarantine

Let me not keep my distance
In the matters of human existence
I refuse to accept the discontent
Facing mutual accompaniment
This time we inhabit is much too shallow
To deem the heretic as the hallow
Let me hold your hand, caress you with kisses
Let me feel your connections and your misses
And when we emerge from this quarantine
We shall have conquered what was unseen

ferro igni

Go forth, young gladiator
Fight the good fight
Go forth and conquer all those
Who douse you with great spite

Though your weapon is quite broken
And your resources near nonexistence
Remember that you have never lost
Your will of unceasing persistence

When the day finally comes
For you to confront that savage beast
Hold your shield tight; your resolve even tighter
And waver not in the very least

As the empyrean artificer's breath
Of Hephaistos transmutes fear to fire
Harness that blaze so you can live
And raise hell to unholy desire

Be quick, and nimble, and commit
Doom slays those who are undone
And those who choose to idly wait
Inevitably become no one

So when the fatal deed is finished
Quench your thirst in the river
Though the flame still burns strong
Your fear is but a shiver

right of way

In the city you can't see the stars
So I turn to the streetlights, instead
Of a more divine celestial navigator
Power that I don't think I can ever
Control by turning on or off or on again
Dreams work in reverse for most people
And by that I mean they are wide awake
When most are asleep
I am not like most people (I'm special)
When the night comes out to the U street bars
And leaves behind traces of willful debauchery
That is when I'm wide awake
I'm searching for my phone I've lost
I'm searching for my wallet I've lost
I'm searching for my purpose
Though I've never really had that one
So I suppose I'm not going to find that in
    the backseat
Of my last Uber driver
But I'll call and text anyways, just to be sure
My friends are all going to be hungover
But tomorrow I'll be as clear as ever
To those who dare to walk in my way

1960

Whoever decided that our life was to be ruled
By 60 seconds was obviously not thinking it through
I mean, tell that to Scott and Steph
Cooking on a butane container a can of refried beans
With a round (or two, or just one more) of dominoes
    before bed
And among the church choir of oaks, loblolly pines
    and hickory trees
I see the images of my life in aortic fantasy and
    fractal brilliance.
Though I've lost my eyesight, my vision
    remains strong
And I hold with diligent tenderness
    my granddaughter
And take up my hourly ration with the fraternity
As I read and ponder my last obituary

my favorite place

Our shadows do not die when we do
The Proof lies on the side of a meadow
Grim faces overlooking a stream where
Deer gather in the mornings and where
Lovers gather to take their selfies in the evenings
And where air sits still in the afternoons
The young and the old look down at this stream of
Unceasing, unending life that carries
The earliest and latest blossoms downstream
Their shadows grow long as the sun grows old
They keep reaching for the water with hope that
  they shall
Be ferried on the petals wept from a cherry tree

telephone call from the universe

There is a poem in which I know only a fragment
I recall it in only the times of shadow
In the brief moment that the moon appears in
    the afternoon
On a walk that I took by myself with others, too
The songs that I like are too much for me
So I hum only the refrain instead
Giving myself only a glimpse of the whole song
Sung by the sparrows who fear nothing, for
They sit on the sidewalk and wonder why we stand
So far away, together in our apartness
United by uncertainty, divided by eternity

ladies in yellow

She stands there, her eyes cast downward
A living goddess walking among mortals
A fallen angel afraid of her own power
As the people push past her, they take little notice
The goddess knows not of how to walk
Her billowing dress flows around her like
Seafoam as water falls from the sky
Downcast with her eyes yet unseeing of the
Times to come for those she protects
And then there was the lady in yellow
Who asked me to take a photo of her
She was obviously unlike the rest of us
And yet, she was so much like me
Her presence dominant, her gaze steady
These are the two ladies in yellow
With graciousness they play their parts
No regard for the beginning -
Just the middle of what they are achieving
And love in their eyes was unceasing
Apparent in their heavy breathing
Should we be indebted to these ladies in yellow?
We look, we ponder.
We dream, we wonder.

this means nothing

I am a dirigible, incorrigible, irritable
Recurring miserable in the disbursement of chaos
Two socks unmatched, unhinged in the color and size
Two lovers telling each other honest lies
Two glowing eyes with the element of surprise
My throne reminds me of royal humanity flushed with
False confusion and survivalist sanity.
And shall I be dancing descending the stairs
To catch the righteous quite unawares?
Do the blind speak well and the deaf observe truly
What happens when you strip away the natural and
Leave only the super to sit in stupor on the
   park bench
Of last night's great unveiling of humanity's
   true nature
As you listen with intent as the birds sing
To the eerie solitude of abandoned spring.
I am a dirge, a scourge, a purged
Whirring comfortable in the divestment of calm
I lay down my crown and join the ranks of
   the emerged.
One sock matched to itself, one lover and one eye.
Give up what I had, for it was never actually mine.

district of ohio

Perhaps we are to meet each other again some day
Not in the places we have met before
But somewhere else in the after
Another Metro stop on the green line that turns to
    red and winds its way down to the underbelly of
    the city
Roaring from within the deep like a belching rusted
    dragon interrupted from its stupor
Perhaps we are all passengers on the same train but
    with different stops
(though same delays and signals)
We have been told that our hearts cannot be close
We have been told that we needed those forty days
    and forty nights
As our ships drifted with Lazarian fever on the seas
    of sorrow
As we watch with wistful eyes to set our feet on
    solid ground
As we see each other stand on the subway silently,
    six steps from safety

girl at the window

The look on my sullen face
Softens as I stand at this place
Let my hair form as shells
As I savor some salty swells
For in looking out, I look within
Swimming in questions of when
Let me stay inside so I can see
The palace of my destiny

called

Let me not waste my time hence
On matters of pure happenstance
Of leaves that fall with the coming of dawn
With life escaping the lips of the wronged
With patience I have sat waiting for answers
Auditioning my thoughts on a stage with no dancers
And I have gone to lands full of dreams
Emerging from my sleep with promises on
    broken wings
With each passing day I grow much younger
I have more wisdom, I have more hunger
Across the ocean to the Galapagos and then
    South Korea
I follow the susurrations of kinetic Medea
And let me slip one small stale baguette
And dip it in boiled milk, letting the concoction set
And I shall savor burnt butter with
    Pigeons Transmogrified
As I listen carefully to a question unreplied

chapter two

The real tragedy was that I didn't love her fully
The way life turned inside out was like
A half-baked piece of bread
Hard on the outside and raw in the middle
And ever so difficult to swallow
My dissatisfaction (or disappointment)
    forever stopped
On the twelve seconds of a clock
Impatience pushed me too soon from this place
And the real tragedy is that we never get to see
    our face
As others see us, we only get a reflection
And even that is false, or is that perhaps more real
So long as we let it destroy us, then we may heal

temporary leave of absence

There are parts to a poem of which I recall only
   a fragment
The gap widening between anxiety and excitement
The half-stolen glance of nose and mouth covered
The forbidden destiny yet to be discovered
The sacred pause of the breath going in and then out
The difference between a whisper and a shout
The strain of my muscles as I am reaching
The tragic gap between love and beseeching
The dying moments of spring turning to fall
The infinite hollow between nothing and all
The artificial lines of the end and the start
The confusion between Nietzche and Descartes
The lilting pitch between lie and untruth
The seconds standing between wisdom and youth
The trembling space betwixt loneliness and solitude
The question of being blunt or being rude
Perhaps I've been mistaken all along
For that fragment is the actual song

studying a new language

I show love by cleaning the dishes
And dwell deep inside your wishes
I turn the water all the way up to hot
And look for continuance rather than not
I spill water, water everywhere
And look to soak up all your fears
I handle used spoons, and forks, and knives
I cut through the layers of all your past lives
I scour the stains so vigorously
As I tackle our struggles so seriously
I let my hands age in the water
And let my bones begin to totter
I show love by granting your wishes
And dwell deep inside your dishes

Let me not my soul lament
When rain darkens our secret covenant
No trace of where the joy went
No joints to keep my spirit unbent
All I see is the world thrown asunder
The answers replaced by dark wonder
Fearful of the impending thunder
And the storm that may put us under
Unmoor that ship and loosen its lashing
Erstwhile the sky is struck by flashing
So worry not about sink nor swim
For we shall ride dreams on a whim

monologue

When a person departs
They set a time
For them to arrive at the start
Of something new
They used to say that when someone dies
A clock stops, so I used to go around
Changing the clocks to buy them more time
But their moment would still arrive
Marked by the sound of a ghostly chime
Listen, listen
Listen to what their life has wrought
In the purpose that they have sought
Was their time here all for naught
Or is there victory in how they fought?
You will discover that time can tell
When the ring echoes of another bell
Find yourself not in hell
But in the heaven of the well.

i, farragut west

I am but a ghost in this city
Walking the streets I used to roam
Every step I have trod on
Feels eerily quite unknown
The passersby on the town
Feel nothing of what I see
Only the signs on a building
Allowed for some vacancy
And when the time came for the rush
I heard no sight and saw no noise
Of souls suspended in equipoise
And out of the corner of my eye
I gathered my own reflection
That ghost which I had became
Stepped into resurrection
Let me not wander this empty place
Feeling rather alone
Allow me instead to heed the voices
Of angels calling me home

singsong

Bird song is a birth song a fight song a love song a word song
Not stuck but strong
Not sing but sung
Not sick but strong
Bird song is my song your song their song our song
Where we tag along
Where we get along
Where we play along
Bird song is a folk song a theme song a torch song a swan song
It is hourlong
It is lifelong
It is agelong

i want poetry

Some day when the history books write of this time
And this chapter is assigned to the younger ones
They'll say that this is the closest we've come to
    world peace
And the most distant away from it, too

Depending on who you read, it was the best of times
It was the worst of times, it was the end of times

I believe during this time everyone was composing
    poetry in their homes
A cacophonous symphony of scattered keys locked
    away in our heads
And the birds sang what we were all singing
    to ourselves
That lost medley of lust blended with love alone
A cocktail unshaken at a party postponed

I watched as the tree outside my window, frames
A place where a man had sat down to rest

And runners passed in and out of the picture
While he remained steady in his gaze
Am I watching him, or is he watching me?
And I'll sit in my rocking chair and tell that story
Of how that man no longer sits there
And the life I gave to gulp down fresh air

left turn

Maybe well-being has another meaning than the
    surface level truth
Just like you may look into the bottom of a well and
    find that it has no end
The wisping echo of a bird chirp buried
And a flame half past hurried
With little ceremony
With little warning
With little sound
Dissipating disappearance suspended
On the edge of Occam's Razor
And the blade of delicate grass that divides dreams
    from nightmares
They should look down
They should look deep
Into that hole in the ground
For they will discover to great delight
That the fire and phoenix have survived the night

admission

I need silence, not music today
To guide my consciousness on the way
Through the channel of my despair
Formed as tiny droplets in the air
And lo did that divine melody persist
To the chagrin of my exorcist
Those demons lifeless in the deep abyss
Emerging to create a world amiss
This reality is all I have ever known
A hellish landscape of destroyed Rome
The lights long buried by the night
The lost traveler hidden out of sight

Walk with me instead on this path
Shy not away from grief and from wrath
Remember your lessons as a child
Tame the human by being wild
Free the tiger pacing in its cage
Let its anger run unrestrained
For one way exists to ownership
A loving hug, not a lashing whip
We are not unalike, you and I
In forgetting to ask how instead of why
Let that question remain a statement
Shed forever your moral raiment

The silver fox, the impish hare
I happened upon in the forest
Both paused at me with questioning
As if they were intent on listening
That fox stood steady like a monolith
An immortalized mortal dweller
That hare had hurried through the wood
For survival is always better
And I, half-starved in my journey
Spared my soul of innocence
As the hare escaped with nimbleness

found

There are many ways of getting somewhere
But only one way of staying still
It's a destination that you won't reach
Through sheer force of one's will

They ask me for directions, often
And do to themselves much violence
Yet all they really had to do
Was sit and listen to the silence

Destiny is not a goal or place
Where there is a stop or start
Destiny is the now and here
Look within, feel your heart

The fork in the road is an illusion
The choice is made a lie
Why would you walk, run, crawl or skip
When you could really fly?

So if you are searching, searching for ease
Stop in your tracks and start to breathe

the cafe

There's a young girl looking in at me
Through the closed door of my store
She looks at me with wistful eyes
And a look forlorn
I have never looked out for several years
Ever since that Act
Where I realized there was betrayal
Of so many different facts
She puts her hands against the glass
Her fingers splayed out against the pane
She wants to come inside and wonders
If her efforts are in vain
This little girl, that balancing act
Those lies foretold, that faithless fact
I want to exit from my soliloquy
And welcome her back in
Yet to do so would cause me great pain
And may even be a sin
Last night was Wednesday and today is not
And tomorrow is already past
When that little girl leaves me behind
Then I will be the last

satellite

Lights exist in many forms in this city
A running advertisement, not even the driver knows
How to get to where you want to be, eventually
And sirens, blinding bulbs of exploding colors
Whether it means trouble or safety depends on how
    close you stand
The light of the bachelorette television screen
At 4:30 AM I watch with them
Across the street from where I sit and ask myself
What happens during the nights that flash starting
    green and stopping red
To no one who is fast asleep
One, two, three
In a blink
A switch flipped
A flash indistinct

home

Home is the bottom of an ocean
That has never seen the sun
A tranquility like the sky
Tumultuous tides passing by

I have already both arrived and left
My dreams bereft of a step to step
A widowed window not fully blinded
An endless hallway continuously winded

May we suspend ourselves in liquid space
As we dust away memories once erased

a poem revised

Writing poetry sometimes is like a recipe
With implied blanks that only the chef can see
There's adding and math but no subtraction
Only using measurements of some abstraction
A recipe contains within the sign of the times
A lyric holds no meaning unless it rhymes
And if we burn it then shall we throw it away?
Should we discard the poem for a syllable astray?
Some people claim that they are crummy cooks
To this I say that they have the wrong books
The best path to creation is to delight in the process
Even if you sometimes screw up the sauces
And whether it tastes good in their mouths,
   who cares
As long as they're hungry, they'll stay in their chairs

order #66

OK, so we have always worn masks
They're just on the surface now
And maybe I shouldn't say this aloud
But I think there's always been some kind of dis-ease
Lingering beneath the surface
And I know that I might sound odd
Yet it's better than being even more afraid
Of each new edict that tries to contain
Something that we don't have control over

I knew that there was trouble when they closed
	the churches
When those who preach fervently of daily bread
Decided to remain home instead
And if we cover our mouths with a fabric bound
	and gag
Are we silencing ourselves or protesting with silence

We sit still and pray with daily dread
I rise from my knees and demand instead to see
	your face
And hear your voice for real
And cry nay to that covering
My humble request: stand at the pulpit
	and sermonize
How to bring fear to its demise

understatement

You haven't lived until you've tried making poetry
Making love between the lines
Making war between the lies
Making peace between the sighs
Looking out the window as you accept that not all of
    your words hold meaning
At least not right now, anyway
And that you must practice working
    within constraints
Divisions drawn firmly by complaints
Never mind that you always mind what other
    minds think
Write your poetry, anyway, with a knowing wink

There are stories that I invent in my head
That fill me with an impending sense of dread
This galaxy of infinite, undying dimensions
Those characters of phantom unmentions

And my mug draws one too many rings
Overlapping regions of things within things
The mystery reader deciphering coffee grounds
At loss for which prophecy may be found

And I paint with false colors in a layer of dust
Inspecting my surface closely, misdirecting my trust
An hourglass half full cannot tell the time
Life must be turned upside down, sometime

I peel away pages pressed against my head
No longer at a loss for what's up ahead
I find my pen, I start to hastily write
For dreams cannot be seen when you have sight

conjuring

Opposite of a judge
Able to make ideas visible, invisibly
A true magician in all of the senses
An indomitable spirit
A soul undiminished
In the shadow of Death
Denied consent
Demons, howling in protest
She, reincarnated as revenant

cruising altitude: thirty-four thousand feet

We sit, our seatbelts buckled
In two neat rows
And as two lovers hold hands across the aisle
I sit as a witness of their holy matrimony.
They were preparing to rise from the earth
Together.
And in that moment, I saw life in their hands.
Fingers forming a raft in the narrow strait between
    waves of people
Flesh touching in the quiet alley of a sleepy but sad
    romantic road
The kind covered in cobblestones that would stumble
    your feet.
And the caress of fingertips in the empty aisle of an
    organic hipster store –
A quiet respite from the throngs of hungry and
    prying eyes.
I saw their soul clasped together
In moments where the darkness fell
Into the hallowed earth and birthed a constellation
    of galaxies
Stretching far, far into the abyss above.
And at cruising altitude, they finally let go
Two hearts sitting next to each other
Content and safe in the knowledge
Of being up in the air.

unexpectation

I never left the deep down room
Of my sheltered mind
I feared that I would lose
What I thought was a rhyme
And so I watch people pass day by day
And hesitate with a knock
Only to be swept away
From the broken lot
Until one day someone came to my place
And how she did this I do not know
But I woke up to a delightful breeze
And emerged through an open window
If the door is shut and no one left behind
So be it if it means the freedom from the mind

i could sit on the couch and listen to music all day

What is less and what is more
Is a question of what's in store
Do we look through with fear
Or do we soldier on with ongoing cheer?
Too often we think that we cannot
Be until we obtain a thing that was sought.
And is it true that the past is unfair
To those who dare to trust thin air?
Invisibility is a skill I know well
How I learned it, I cannot tell
I grow old, I grow old
But until I die, I will be bold.
So pay attention the next time you look
For the joy that life has took,
Since you know me and I know you
We shall see each other through.

alignment

A line.
What does it mean?
A line that you dared not cross, because you didn't know what was on the other side.
A line that you stood in quietly, because you were told to.
A line that became a box, which you lived in, because you believed it was safe.
A line that said, "Keep out."
"Stop."
"Don't let me in."

When you draw a line, do you draw it straight?
Linear, or does it squiggle
And zig zag ever so slightly to the left?
I used to think that a line had to be in one direction
Always looking forward
Always rooted to a point in the past
But struggling to get to the future.
And it meant division.
Between my heart and mind.

A line that carved itself into my chest
One that I couldn't move or erase
And it stayed there
Daring me to cross, because it knew that I wouldn't.

A line meant something to me then
And different to me now.

It's a ray of light instead.
    And a rotating entity that becomes
        the sun,
            More rounded, and more whole
        That was when I discovered
    Alignment
For me

snapshot

When you see a photograph
Does it fill you with despair
Looking at a memory realized
Out of the pale thin air
Do you dare look into the eye
Which can see more than you can think
Or will you let your fears take hold
And end on a permanent blink?
I work to capture the beauty inside
But I only have found you
The life lived but somewhat dead
For the dreams that didn't come true
If we take a shot and attempt
To see the next frame of light
Should we be afraid of what we find
Or what passes our able sight
And in the night would you expose
The film of your fragile soul
Or would you stay in the dark
And love only what was untold
Let me use the shutter flash
Not to blind but let you see
Let me bring you into the light
And tell you it was me

in transport

They always say from dust to dust,
But I wonder about the in between
What of the stories of great delight
And of the wonder yet unseen?
As the sparrow flies through the sun,
And settles in the dawn
Then the owl coos softly at the moon,
And greets me with a yawn.
That's when I heard the caw of death
But I dared not respond with song
For I have died not once but twice
And been there all along.
Watch me in the still of night
When the ripple glows
Watch me in the will of might
When the moonlight grows
If hope is a thing made from feather
As a soul once said
The best question is not whether
But if you would instead.

ask me for my name (part 2)

Ask me for my name
On my first day of school
For twelve years
And I'll tell you my nickname instead
Ask me when I say I'm from down South but you
    don't believe me
Because someone with my name couldn't possibly
    be American
Ask me when you interview me
And assume what I'm capable of
Ask me when I do a good deed
Because that's what I've been taught
To think of others above myself
And never to see my own individual identity as
    something to be valued
Or to be the recipient of an "I love you"
Ask me what my name means
And I'll tell you it means sunshine
It means being an adult before you're ready
It means nights alone
It means not understanding but having
    to understand
In a world that doesn't understand you

flight patterns

Climb Out
Late night Denver shift
Mop away the travel dirt
Last flight out tonight

Base Leg
Climbing is easy
Looking upwards at the sky
Descending is hard

Final Approach
Elevation change
Feel your heart pound and sing
Summit climb at last

doors opening on the right

Somerville Drive
Shady Grove metro
A common destination
But different stops

Connecticut Avenue
Subway lipstick
Red line train
Single track only

Scott Circle
The winter thaw
Rolled up sleeves
Revealing a bit more

action item #2

First Course

Delight in the practice itself
Like a child enjoying an ice cream cone in
    the summer
That's how I want to paint
Licking all around the rounded edges of a
    sweet concoction
Sugary cream dripping
Through my fingers
An accidental Pollock
God took almost seven days, so what is it to me
If I take a second scoop from eternity

Second Course

Focus, not distraction
Change, not maladaptation

Breath, not strangulation
Gentle, not domination

Revision, not demolition
Abundance, not starvation

Stillness, not hesitation
Truth, not distortion

Revenant, not expiration
Progress, not perfection

birdsong #2

Bird song is a love song, a fight song, a heart strung
Across the branches that sing to the howling wind
A key signature set to mysterious notes left
By spirits
In the morning I wake up to the sound of vegetal
    notes of nutty traffic
And the brightness of commuters in the city
And that familiar tone of earthy greatness at the back
    of my throat
With floral eighteenths on the sixteenth floor
Heights of enormous calamities move me through
    the shadows
Eyes open and shut from the blinding darkness in
    the caverns of light
And so I look not with them or for them anymore, no I
    simply listen
As the soft flutter of wings reaches a crescendo in
    the sky

the second rain

I don't ever cry twice
The way the sun shines through the leaves
Commands me to do so - and besides the trees
 need their
Crying turn, too, when they feel wet and cold and
Like me turn up the collars of their raincoat around
 their ears
And try to face the storm bravely
The moaning of yearning as their tears splash in
 my face
I'm turning around now, okay? Wrong way, good day —
Sir, catch the rain with the palm of your hand
Gaze intently upwards and let that rain strike
 your face
Twice
First on your virtue
And then on your vice

it's all about balance

A photograph is an epitaph of the past
A moment forced to last through a forced smile
That travels the miles through space; a memory
Inscribed on your face that glancing sideways stare
When you wouldn't dare to reach past the
Present and see what was to come so you
Live instead undone by the thoughts of someone
Ceaseless and ceasing, dying and dreaming and yet
Breathless and breathing as rage builds like a
    pacing beast
Waiting for a feast of your insecurities and depression
Laid before you in a devastating procession —
I implored you
Once to let the beast be free and true, yet you
    refused and
What am I to do but let you be you and to let
The light penetrate truth

unoccupation

When they told us that we had to leave our schools
Effective immediately tomorrow
I rushed home as fast as I could
I didn't realize that the shortages would occur
    so swiftly
Though I should have paid more attention to what
    the newspapers said
And as the guns rolled down the streets
I remembered where my friend Maria and I used
    to play
As I listened to Mother sobbing quietly in the
    next room
And every day is a day of waiting for our turn
As unoccupied coffee shops, restaurants, hotels, and
    bars stare blankly
And we bring our furniture back inside
And we close our doors and windows and mouths
    and eyes
Even though it is spring and my neighbors Helga
    and Theodore
Still come outside every day to work on their garden
And I skip rope, sometimes, when the bells still sound
And I skip rope, sometimes, when the birds still sing
And I skip rope, sometimes, when the bombs
    still scream
Even though it is spring and my friends Helga
    and Theodore
Stopped coming outside
Dirty snow falling, falling from the sky as the city
    hangs with eerie silence
And my Mother's makeup streaks like a scar
And that OPEN sign on the bakery that used to serve
    me sweet bread tells no time
Unoccupied — undone, unheard, unfinished, unwon,
    unbecome, unless

Would there be a reset or a return
Or do I need to watch with shyness
As a man tilts his head back to smell a single rose
    through that aghast mask
And keeps the roses to himself, because I dare
    not ask?

Gingko   bread
Cypress   eggs
Oak   milk
Maples   honey
(check for flour but don't expect any)
Cherry   soda
Wisteria   Chicken
Magnolia oranges

That blue sky, unoccupied
No one else here is unoccupied
Helga and Theodore, unoccupied
Smashed right palm of a statue, unoccupied
And my Mother seems unoccupied
Vacant in her thoughts, absent in her actions
And I want to step defiant into that space as our
    freedoms are erased
Unacceptable, unlawful, untruthful, unstoppable,
    unforgettable, unimaginable, undefeated

Gingko, Cypress, Oak, Maple, Cherry, Wisteria
Bread, Egg, Milk, Honey, Soda, Chicken, Oranges
No one can accuse me of not having tried
When I go to bed hungry, but oddly satisfied

can you hear me?

You can't possibly claim to know me
Because I don't even know myself
I am not some book to be read
And ignominiously stored away on a shelf
You can't possibly claim to own me
Where I must cede to you all control
I'm not as helpless as you think
I carry a laser beam in my soul
You can't possibly claim to show me
The right way to live this second life
When the seas that you sail are so tumultuous
So full of struggle and strife
You can't possibly claim to bestow me
With any of your so-called wisdom
For I can spot in an instant
The illusion of your so-called kingdom

I am in charge of my journey; I am in charge of my fate
If the time is right, I'll let you participate.

blank spaces

Brushed hair
Homeless face
Painful memory
Never erased
Bags of groceries
An open hand
Disconnection
Damp palms
Together
And not
Hearts dropped
On the sidewalk

springtime in the city

Golden haiku
Silver quality —
New life
New allergy —
Chirping birds
Stolen grass —
Delayed at work
Expired Metro pass —

fo(u)r hours on end

When you realize that you are worthy enough
Then you realize that you don't need to hold up half
    the sky
And that you can throw away that apple core
And the earth pushes you up, instead of pulling
    you down
You experience a lightening of the load
A sinking of the sand
A releasing of regret
And you become the smallest of the baobab seeds
And the infinite of the infinitesimal
How simple was it for Atlas to set down his burden
And trust that there was an even larger Heaven to
    hold up space?
It was the belief that he should suffer that made it so.
Let the ego shout, let it let out its air —
I'll be light as the breeze, I'll be cutting off my hair.
And I'll lay down and let the flowers grow over me,
Not dead or alive, but simply free.

one fish, two fish (for alicia)

Depressed, stressed, but still well dressed
Would you say that our society is obsessed
With the idea of likes, and loves, and follows?
Cemented to our devices
Trapped by our crises
I want the noise to stop.
But the notifications keep coming
Swipe right to see what's left of our generation
Too late to pull back a presupposed revolution
You see I wore a mask already a long time ago
No one asked me to cover up my lies
To take nothing by surprise
And I thought, I thought I was being so wise
Hiding my mouth, nose, and eyes.
Compromise. Realized. And before you know it
No one knows when you show it.
When you become helpless as you undress
Your mask is weary of wearing you down and around
    and sideways
You want to curse but you're swearing
That you'll never let them see that face, erased.
Unless, unless, unless
There is another heart out there
Avoiding the daggers of judgmental stares
Catching you, unprepared, and they wipe away
Those tears and pull back your unkempt hair
Life's a game of truths — and not of dares.

master sun

They say that I'm being partial
When I call my battle martial
No time to negotiate, when lives are at stake
They say that I'm forgetting the how
When I focus on the now
No mind to distract, when I'm locked in combat
They say that I'm doing the impossible
When I see myself as unstoppable
No place to hesitate, when death premeditates
Let life destroy and tear you apart
Suffer neither victory nor loss
Because we know
Fighting is Art

wisdom of the crowd

Can we trust what we can see
By a mind illuminated by a killer bee
With the poison of the dagger bestowed
Nature takes back what was rightfully owed
And is it the truth if everybody lies
Or is our winking more of a disguise
We look for answers with wondering mystery
And bleed our hearts with pondering history
Finding nothing on this wretched earth
I raised my head to the stars that gave us birth
And there I find the beast named Rangifer
In the face of Orion quite undeterred
And I, standing in balance, between two moons
Sing with the bluebirds their final tunes

my renaissance

Where the magic happens is a place of in-betweens
Of the golden ratio between the end and the means
A snap of the fingers and a flick of the wrist
The sly hand gestures of an illusionist
A wave washing over lines in the sand
A floating blade hanging by a strand
An unreal mirage created through lies
Tricks played upon our blinded eyes
And now for my final disappearing act
I question the perception you see as Fact

not yet/unless

I am
The second to last
The penultimate omega
The final inhale
The closing bodega
The baton suspended before applause
The subject of a predicate clause
The moon in wane
The almost set quiche lorraine
The piece of bread mostly stale
The spoon in the drawer
The gasping wail
The ripple in the sand
The time for naught
The passing glance never caught

acknowledgements

To David,
who patiently listened to almost all my poems before morning coffee.

To Emily,
for being the light and laughter of my life.

To Mom and Dad,
for telling me that I'm a great writer. I love you.

To Samantha and Maggie,
for all of your hugs and snuggles.

To Dave, Marisa, and Casey,
for coaching me through my spiritual and professional transformations.

To Shelley,
for teaching me how to read and write English.

To Veronica,
for answering all my emails promptly and designing a beautiful book.

To my friends – past, present, and future – for celebrating my weirdness.

Tracy Huang is a Chinese-American poet living in Washington, D.C. She attended Amherst College and New York University School of Law. She likes to tell the truth, but tell it slant.

www.ingramcontent.com/pod-product-compliance
Lightning Source LLC
Chambersburg PA
CBHW042326150426
43192CB00004B/125